283694

50 Quick and Easy Ways to Prepare for Ofsted

By Mike Gershon

D1331457

Text Copyright © 2014 Mike Gershon

All Rights Reserved

About the Author

Mike Gershon is a teacher, trainer and writer. He is the author of twenty books on teaching, learning and education, including a number of bestsellers, as well as the co-author of one other. Mike's online resources have been viewed and downloaded more than 2.5 million times by teachers in over 180 countries and territories. He is a regular contributor to the Times Educational Supplement and has created a series of electronic CPD guides for TES PRO. Find out more, get in touch and download free resources at www.mikegershon.com

Training and Consultancy

Mike is an expert trainer whose sessions have received acclaim from teachers across England. Recent bookings include:

- *Improving Literacy Levels in Every Classroom*, St Leonard's Academy, Sussex

- *Growth Mindsets, Effective Marking and Feedback* Ash Manor School, Aldershot

- *Effective Differentiation,* Tri-Borough Alternative Provision (TBAP), London

Mike also works as a consultant, advising on teaching and learning and creating bespoke materials for schools. Recent work includes:

- *Developing and Facilitating Independent Learning,* Chipping Norton School, Oxfordshire

- *Differentiation In-Service Training,* Charles Darwin School, Kent

If you would like speak to Mike about the services he can offer your school, please get in touch by email: mike@mikegershon.com

UCB
283694

Other Works from the Same Authors

Available to buy now on Amazon:

How to use Differentiation in the Classroom: The Complete Guide

How to use Assessment for Learning in the Classroom: The Complete Guide

How to use Questioning in the Classroom: The Complete Guide

How to use Discussion in the Classroom: The Complete Guide

How to Teach EAL Students in the Classroom: The Complete Guide

More Secondary Starters and Plenaries

Secondary Starters and Plenaries: History

Teach Now! History: Becoming a Great History Teacher

The Growth Mindset Pocketbook (with Professor Barry Hymer)

How to be Outstanding in the Classroom

Also available to buy now on Amazon, the entire 'Quick 50' Series:

50 Quick and Brilliant Teaching Ideas

50 Quick and Brilliant Teaching Techniques

50 Quick and Easy Lesson Activities

50 Quick Ways to Help Your Students Secure A and B Grades at GCSE

50 Quick Ways to Help Your Students Think, Learn, and Use Their Brains Brilliantly

50 Quick Ways to Motivate and Engage Your Students

50 Quick Ways to Outstanding Teaching

50 Quick Ways to Perfect Behaviour Management

50 Quick and Brilliant Teaching Games

50 Quick and Easy Ways to Outstanding Group Work

50 Quick and Easy Ways to Prepare for Ofsted

50 Quick and Easy Ways Leaders can Prepare for Ofsted

About the Series

The 'Quick 50' series was born out of a desire to provide teachers with practical, tried and tested ideas, activities, strategies and techniques which would help them to teach brilliant lessons, raise achievement and engage and inspire their students.

Every title in the series distils great teaching wisdom into fifty bite-sized chunks. These are easy to digest and easy to apply – perfect for the busy teacher who wants to develop their practice and support their students.

Acknowledgements

As ever I must thank all the fantastic colleagues and students I have worked with over the years, first while training at the Institute of Education, Central Foundation Girls' School and Nower Hill High School and subsequently while working at Pimlico Academy and King Edward VI School in Bury St Edmunds.

Thanks also to Alison and Andrew Metcalfe for a great place to write and finally to Gordon at KallKwik for help with the covers.

Table of Contents

Introduction

Know Your School's Priorities

Connect the Priorities to Your Own Practice

Why does the school have these priorities?

Know Your Own Priorities

Know Your Team's Priorities

Contextual Seating Plans

Data Context Sheets

Use Data to Inform Your Planning

Track Student Progress and Targets in Student Books

Be Aware of Specific Groups of Students

Train Your Students in Routines

Where would you like an observer to sit?

Ask yourself what you're not doing that you could be doing

Observe Yourself

Look at Students' Books

Plan for Progress

Differentiate

There's No Single Right Way

Make Learning Happen

Be Clear

Ensure All Your Marking is Up-To-Date

Mark Carefully and with Purpose

Formative Marking

Track Comments and Responses

Give Students a Chance to Respond to and Implement Targets

Make Sure Students Know Where They're Going

Print Off Your Mark Book

Identify How to Show Progress

Reflective Paragraphs

Targets and Reflections in the Same Piece of Work

Pupil Premium Students

Students on Free School Meals

Students for who English is and Additional Language

Students who are on the SEN Register

Students who are Gifted and Talented

Wall Displays

Health and Safety

Can you move around with ease?

Tinker with your Seating Plans

Have a Back-Up!

Ofsted.gov.uk

The Current Inspection Framework

Good Practice Guides

Specific Guidance

Outstanding Inspection Reports

Relax

If you're prepared, then you're prepared

Speak to Colleagues

Know Your Strengths (And Play to Them)

It's All About Learning and Progress

A Brief Request

Introduction

Welcome to '50 Quick and Easy Ways to Prepare for Ofsted.'

This book is all about the things you can do to prepare for an Ofsted inspection. It provides practical advice, strategies and ideas you can implement to make sure you are well-set for any inspection. It will aid you in doing the best job possible for your students.

Of course, the results of an inspection depend on the judgements the inspectors make. This book makes no claims that it will help you to achieve a specific grade.

What it does offer though, is suggestions on how to prepare, the kind of things you need to think about and the various resources which are out there waiting to be used.

The focus is practical throughout. Every entry offers something tangible you can do or use to help prepare yourself, your students and your teaching.

And the overall aim is simple: to help you to prepare as effectively as possible for any upcoming visits you might have from Ofsted.

So read on and enjoy; and if you do get inspected, good luck!

Know Your School's Priorities

01 Every school seeks to improve. Every school should seek to improve. As such, every school has priorities for development. Usually, these will be laid out in your institution's school development plan.

It is important to know your school's priorities at all times. This is so that you can contribute to them, whatever your role.

When Ofsted come in, they may ask you about the school's priorities. If you have familiarised yourself with these, you can talk about them. In fact, you could even bring them up yourself, explaining to an inspector who is observing you how what you are doing ties into the school's overall drive for improvement.

Connect the Priorities to Your Own Practice

02 Connecting the school's priorities to your own practice is not only a good thing to do in and of itself, but it also illustrates to any inspector the joined up thinking which permeates your school (as well as your own professionalism).

We can exemplify this point by looking at the converse. Imagine that one of your school's priorities is raising achievement for pupils on free school meals. Now, if an inspector observes you or speaks to you about your teaching and you make no mention whatsoever of this (either verbally or in any documentation) you are failing to convey the reality of what you are doing.

Making explicit the connection between the school's priorities and your own practice will always be a positive thing you can do.

Why does the school have these priorities?

03 Ideally, you want to be in a position where you can explain why the school has the priorities it has, as well as how you are connecting these to your own practice.

This is simply because it is always better to know why something exists than to not know. If we know, we can talk knowledgably about it. If we don't, we can't.

If you are unsure why your school has certain priorities, speak to a senior leader. Ask them to give you a brief summary of the reasons behind the priorities. You could even turn this into a crib sheet to be passed around the whole staff body (but only once they have signed it off, of course!).

Know Your Own Priorities

04 The next thing to think about is your own priorities.

Ask yourself what your focus is with the different classes you teach. This is something you will know implicitly and which you will use every day to inform your practice. However, making it explicit and getting it clear in your mind will make life easier for you if you are observed or have to speak to one of the inspection team.

As teachers, we make professional decisions based on reasoning and evidence. Drawing this reasoning and evidence to the front of your mind will help you to articulate the priorities which underpin your work.

Know Your Team's Priorities

05 In school we are all part of a team and often we are part of multiple teams. Knowing the priorities of the teams of which you are a part is good practice. It allows you to work effectively as a member of those teams, to contribute to their success and to work in unison with your colleagues.

It might be that, during the inspection, no one asks you about your team's priorities. But why take that risk? Better to prepare thoroughly than risk not being able to show the best side of your professional self.

If you are unsure of your team's priorities, speak to your team leader. If you are the team leader, identify the underlying priorities which have been guiding you thus far and communicate these to your colleagues.

Contextual Seating Plans

06 As you will have noted, this book is about preparing for Ofsted but it is also about general best practice. The two things go hand in hand. Contextual seating plans are another example of this.

Seating plans demonstrate that you know your students, that you have placed them in the class with clear consideration of their learning and that you have started differentiating before pupils even enter the room.

A contextual seating plan means you include tags indicating things such as SEN, FSM, EAL, G and T and Pupil Premium. Some teachers also like to include current attainment levels and even brief notes where appropriate.

Data Context Sheets

07 A data context sheet gives an observer a sense of where the class is at, who is in the class and the kind of learning which has been taking place prior to the current lesson.

If your school has a preferred format for data context sheets, use that. Otherwise, you should create your own (or search on www.tes.co.uk to see if someone has uploaded one you feel you can use).

On your sheet you should indicate the gender make-up of the class, the number of FSM, EAL, SEN, G and T and Pupil Premium students, prior achievement levels, a brief summary of what students have been learning and an indication of what they will learn during the current lesson.

Here you are doing three things. First, you are showing that you are prepared, organised and that you know your class. Second, you are helping the observer to understand the class. Third, you are making it easier for them to judge whether progress takes place in your lesson or not.

As an aside, some teachers like to supplement a data context sheet with a print out of their mark book or other electronic assessment data (such as that stored on SIMS or Go4Schools).

Use Data to Inform Your Planning

08 It is good to use data to inform your planning. This is because it helps you to plan lessons which are specific to the students you teach. It also makes it more likely that you will be meeting the needs of all your learners. In turn, this will increase the likelihood that all pupils will make excellent progress.

If you don't already use data to inform your planning, I would recommend you take the step. Data also includes all that information you elicit from your pupils while you are teaching.

You can draw the inspector's attention to examples of how you have used data to inform your planning. At the same time, if you have done this systematically, it should be quite clear to anyone who watches you teach.

Track Student Progress and Targets in Student Books

09 Regardless of whether you think you will be inspected or not, you should track student progress and targets – both in your mark book and in their books. If you don't, how can you or they know if learning is taking place and progress is being made? Admittedly, we can see the results but, really, this needs to be accompanied by a permanent record.

The great advantage of tracking progress and targets in student books is that pupils then have the means to regulate and take ownership of their own learning.

A simple technique involves placing a pro-forma at the start of students' books and then recording your formative feedback here. This makes the feedback easier to find than if it is scattered throughout the book.

Be Aware of Specific Groups of Students

10 Specific groups of students include:

- Students with a special educational need (SEN)

- Students on free school meals (FSM)

- Students who speak English as an additional language (EAL)

- Students who have been designated as gifted and talented (G and T)

- Students who are on the pupil premium register (PP)

It can also include groups of students based on cultural, gender or class factors. For example, your school might be trying to raise the achievement of white, working-class boys. If this is so, it is another group of which you need to be aware.

Thinking about different groups of students means planning and differentiating in order to meet their needs. This is good practice and can be communicated to inspectors verbally, through your teaching or through documents such as seating plans and data context sheets.

Train Your Students in Routines

11 Training your students in routines minimises disruption, makes your life easier and helps lessons to run more smoothly. It also sends out a general message about how we are all working together in pursuit of a shared goal (learning).

Examples of routines in which you can train pupils include:

- The start of lessons

- Specific activity types

- Transitions between activities

- Peer- and self-assessment procedures

- The end of lessons

If you train students in routines, all this work of making things run smoothly will have been done in advance, allowing you to concentrate solely on your teaching when the inspectors are in.

Where would you like an observer to sit?

12 This question is worth addressing because it may be that a suitable answer presents itself. For example, you might decide that you would like an observer to sit next to a pupil whose behaviour is sometimes difficult. Or, you might want them to sit at the back of the room so you can see where they are.

Of course, an inspector may not sit where you ask; they may not even sit at all!

The point though is that it is better to prepare and rehearse than to find yourself put on the spot. By considering where you would like an observer to sit you have made a decision which you can apply if the situation arises.

Ask yourself what you're not doing that you could be doing

13 Often, when the prospect of an inspection is looming, we can lose focus. This is a familiar reaction when we are faced with something we do not exactly welcome – particularly if that thing is outside of our control.

Asking yourself what you're not doing that you could be doing is a great way to reassert control over the one thing that always remains within your power – you.

If you identify things that you are not doing, then you can make a change. If you run through all the things you are doing and decide that, actually, you're doing everything possible, this knowledge can put you at ease. Either way, the results of asking the question will be positive.

Observe Yourself

14 Whether you realise it or not, the person who has the most knowledge about your teaching is you. Only you experience all your lessons, all your planning, all your marking and all your interactions with your students.

Caught up in the moment, as we often are in school, it is easy to forget this fact. Doing so can make us less reflective and less critically aware.

So, take a few moments while you are teaching to observe yourself. By this, I mean that you should distance yourself from the lesson and try to see objectively what is going on, what you are doing, how you are interacting with pupils and so on.

This isn't easy to do and may take a little bit of practice. The results, however, will be informative and helpful, giving you a clearer sense of where you are at and where you could go next.

Look at Students' Books

15 Invariably, inspectors will look at students' books. This is because they give an indication of the kind of work which is happening in lessons, the level of progress which pupils are making and the type of feedback you are providing.

Look through your students' books and ask yourself the following questions:

- What do these books say about my teaching?

- What do these books say about my marking and feedback?

- What do these books say about the progress pupils in my class are making and the learning that is happening here?

If any of your answers disappoint you, change things. It's never too late.

Of course, it goes without saying that unmarked books give an exceptionally bad impression. Keeping your marking up-to-date is a fundamental element of being a professional. It is a basic expectation any inspector will have of you.

Plan for Progress

16 When delivering any lesson our main aim is securing progress for all our pupils. After all, this is what learning is: being able to do more than you could do before or knowing more than you knew before.

From these points we can deduce that any outstanding lesson will be predicated on the teacher having planned for progress. Ideally, they will have planned for significant progress!

When preparing your lessons at any time, it is good to take this approach. When you know you are going to be inspected, the same is true.

Planning for progress means thinking carefully about how each aspect of the lesson will contribute to pupils making progress. A simple way to ensure this is to use Bloom's Taxonomy. By moving up the taxonomy during individual activities and across the lesson as a whole, you can be almost certain that progress will occur.

For guidance on the taxonomy, see my free resource The Bloom-Buster.

Differentiate

17 Great teaching meets the needs of all students. This isn't easy but it is something we all strive to do. If someone is observing you, they will be looking to see whether all the pupils in your class can make excellent progress; whether or not everybody is in a position to learn.

Differentiation is all about finding practical ways to make the learning accessible and challenging for all pupils.

You can find a wide range of differentiation strategies appropriate for use across the curriculum and the age ranges in my bestselling book, How to use Differentiation in the Classroom: The Complete Guide.

There's No Single Right Way

18 This is important to remember because, when the heat is on and you are anticipating the arrival of the inspection team, it can be tempting to believe that there is a specific, perfect lesson out there that observers want to see.

This is not true.

Michael Cladingbowl, National Director, Schools, provides excellent guidance on this in his Ofsted document 'Why do Ofsted inspectors observe individual lessons and how do they evaluate teaching in schools.' It was released in February 2014 and is a short piece available in PDF and Word format.

I would strongly recommend reading it as it is a very helpful and concise document.

Make Learning Happen

19 In the Michael Cladingbowl document we mentioned in the last entry, we find the following point: "I was speaking to a colleague today, one of Her Majesty's Inspectors. He reminded me it is all about outcomes..." (page 3, http://www.ofsted.gov.uk/resources/why-do-ofsted-inspectors-observe-individual-lessons-and-how-do-they-evaluate-teaching-schools, accessed April 2014).

This is a helpful reminder that the end result is the thing by which judgements are made.

Making learning happen throughout your lessons – including any in which you are observed – will lead to great outcomes for your pupils.

Remember that you can also make learning happen through the marking and feedback you provide verbally and in writing. Inspectors will look at pupils' books. If these demonstrate great outcomes facilitated by high-quality marking and feedback, you will be well on your way to impressing.

Be Clear

20 Clarity is a virtue.

Clarity of communication runs two ways.

First, the clarity with which you communicate with others. Second, the clarity with which you communicate to yourself.

In the latter case, consider how much easier life will be if you can provide a clear and concise rationale for all the decisions you make when planning and teaching.

You will be able to use this knowledge to communicate clearly to others.

Take some time to think about what you are doing with your classes and why. Make your professional judgements and decisions explicit to yourself. You will then be able to communicate these clearly to colleagues, students and inspectors alike.

Ensure All Your Marking is Up-To-Date

21 I have been stressing this point implicitly through the frequent references to marking, feedback and students' books.

If your marking is not up-to-date when the inspectors arrive, this will reflect poorly on you.

More generally, if your marking is not up-to-date then you are not providing pupils with the feedback they need to make great progress.

Up-to-date marking does not mean marking books incessantly. But it does mean ensuring that pupils always know where they are at and what their current target is. This is the fundamental basis of formative feedback (shown to be one of the most significant things a teacher can do to facilitate student progress – see Black et al 2003; Hattie 2012).

Mark Carefully and with Purpose

22 Marking carefully shows attention to detail and a clear desire to support students.

Marking with purpose shows that you are marking with the intention of doing something. That something ought to be helping students to improve and make progress.

If you don't mark carefully, and if no purpose is discernible from your marking, inspectors may question the efficacy of your approach. To what extent, they will wonder, is this marking actually helping pupils to achieve better outcomes?

Personally, I follow the formative marking principle of providing students with three strengths and one target. This target is explained and guidance is given on how to achieve it. When one target is met, we move onto another one and so on.

You might find this model a helpful means by which to ensure your own marking is careful and purposeful. Though I hasten to add that other models are also available!

Formative Marking

23 Formative marking facilitates learning and makes progress happen. Summative does not. Here is a reminder of the difference:

Formative Marking: This essay displays attention to detail and a concerted effort to answer the question. It is clear from your use of specific events and quotes that you have developed a good knowledge of the text. In order to improve, you should include a conclusion in which you state your own opinion on the evidence. This will show the reader that you are capable of making a well-reasoned judgement.

Summative Marking: This essay is a B.

If you use formative marking you will help pupils to make progress. If inspectors see formative marking in your students' books, they will know that you are doing your best to improve outcomes.

Track Comments and Responses

24 Tracking the comments you give and responses students make is a good way to keep on top of formative feedback over time.

You can do this by inserting a tracking sheet in the front of pupils' books, as we mentioned in entry nine.

Furthermore, such a sheet will provide clear evidence that you are marking so as to facilitate progress. If you give space in which students can respond to your comments, this will also demonstrate that you are helping pupils to take control of their own learning and the targets you set them.

Give Students a Chance to Respond to and Implement Targets

25 As we mentioned in the last entry, this is an important element of making students take ownership of their learning.

Here are three simple ways you can help pupils to implement the targets you set them:

- At the start of a piece of work, ask students to write their target. When they finish, ask them to write a paragraph explaining how they have put this target into practice.

- After marking a set of books, begin the next lesson with that class by setting aside time in which they can respond to and then practise their targets.

- At the start of every lesson, ask pupils to write a sentence or two reflecting on how close they are to meeting their targets.

Make Sure Students Know Where They're Going

26 This could be in terms of a specific grade for which they are aiming, the current target they are seeking to meet, the wider purpose of the work they are doing, or all three things. In any case, if pupils do not know where they are going then they are less likely to be motivated or engaged.

Furthermore, it reflects well on you as a teacher if, when asked by an inspector what they are doing and what sort of progress they are making, pupils can give a sound answer or point to some tangible evidence.

This is another reason why formative feedback and tracker sheets are good. They communicate clearly to pupils where they are heading and also act as a reference point to which students can refer if questioned.

Print Off Your Mark Book

27 We mentioned this briefly in entry seven. Here, we return to the point in order to illustrate the potential benefits.

Printing off a copy of your mark book (or making a photocopy if you use a physical mark book) means the inspector has the same assessment data as you. This makes it easier for them to look at and analyse your class as they will have a better understanding of their starting point (and therefore of whether or not pupils are making progress).

If the inspector declines your offer of a copy of your mark book, so be it. You will have lost nothing. If they do take a copy, however, you will have provided them with specific, relevant, contextual information which could prove most valuable.

Identify How to Show Progress

28 One of the differences we feel when we are being observed is the need to show explicitly what is happening in terms of learning. This differs from a normal lesson where we can use our close knowledge of the class, as well as the wider context, to identify the learning which is going on.

In preparation for being observed then, you might like to think about a couple of ways in which you can show progress. Here are three examples to get you going:

- Use a mini-plenary in which pupils can demonstrate their learning.

- Refer to success criteria or lesson objectives and review with your students when and whether these have been met.

- Identify a tangible thing that students will be able to do as a result of their learning. Have them do this as part of the lesson (for example, write a more concise summary of a piece of non-fiction writing).

Reflective Paragraphs

29 Reflective paragraphs are another way in which to show progress. They are a form of self-assessment.

At the end of a task or a piece of work, ask students to write a reflection identifying:

- What they can do now that they couldn't do before

- How they have made progress

- How they have attempted to put their target into practice

You might even preface the self-assessment with a brief paired discussion during which students discuss these three points with a partner.

Of course, it is no good just introducing an approach like this on the week that Ofsted come into your school. Ideally, you should embed it in what you do so that when the inspectors arrive, you are already using excellent practice.

Targets and Reflections in the Same Piece of Work

30 We mentioned this in entry twenty-five. I just want to return to it here because it is an approach I have found to be really effective in my own teaching. In addition, it will clearly illustrate to any observer how important targets and progress are in your classroom.

Ask students to write their target at the start of a piece of work.

They should then aim to implement this target during that piece of work.

And, finally, they should write a reflection analysing the results of what they have done.

As you can see, this method is inherently supportive of positive outcomes and the facilitation of progress. Pupils (who sometimes need to be reminded at each stage of the process) cannot but help think critically about what they need to do to improve.

Pupil Premium Students

31 We turn our attention now to some of the groups of students first outlined in entries six and seven.

Pupil premium students are those students for whom your school receives additional money. This policy was introduced by the coalition government. The students identified as pupil premium are from disadvantaged backgrounds.

Knowing who your pupil premium students are and being able to show how you can support them is important. The inspection framework was revised in 2013 so as to include provision for reporting on the attainment and progress of disadvantaged students who attract the payment.

Students on Free School Meals

32 Students on free school meals are those pupils who receive a school dinner for free. They are from economically disadvantaged backgrounds. The free school meal is a government measure designed to help these students and their families.

With that said, universal free school meals are to be introduced for pupils in reception, year 1 and year 2 from September 2014.

Inspection teams look at the attainment of FSM pupils in a school. The purpose is to see if the school is doing enough to bridge the attainment gap which traditionally exists between this group of pupils and their peers.

So, as with pupil premium students, be aware which of your students are on free school meals and what you are doing to ensure they are making the best progress possible.

Students for who English is and Additional Language

33 Students for who English is an additional language are a broad group. The group ranges from pupils who speak perfect or near-perfect English, akin to that of a native speaker, to those who speak not a word. As such, EAL pupils are best seen as belonging to a continuum of effective English language use.

Ensure you are aware of who the EAL learners are in your classes. You should have strategies in place for supporting these pupils and helping them to learn regardless of their language status.

For practical strategies, activities and techniques with which to support EAL learners, see my free resource The EAL Toolkit and my book, How to Teach EAL Students in the Classroom: The Complete Guide.

Students who are on the SEN Register

34 Students with a special educational need will be on your school's SEN register. This should be freely available to staff, either electronically or as a physical document.

You should know of any pupil who is SEN in the classes you teach and you should have strategies in place to support these learners. As with other groups, Ofsted will look to see whether the school is doing enough to ensure that excellent outcomes and significant progress are being achieved.

If you are unsure about how to support SEN learners, speak to your SENCO or another member of the SEN team. Alternatively, contact fellow teachers who also teach the pupil(s) in question and ask them what they have found to be effective.

Students who are Gifted and Talented

35 Schools are expected to identify pupils in each year group who are deemed gifted and talented. The onus is then on schools to secure excellent outcomes for these students, not least by stretching and challenging their thinking.

As with the other groups mentioned, you should identify which of the pupils you teach are on your school's G and T register. Having done this, you should assess what you can do to support them in your lessons.

For a range of practical ideas on stretching and challenging learners, see my free resource The Challenge Toolkit.

Wall Displays

36 Wall displays are a part of your classroom. They will be noticed. The extent to which they are taken into consideration by inspectors is unknown. However, a positive, well-looked after room in which wall displays support learning and progress is inherently better than the opposite.

Here are some ideas for effective wall displays:

- Examples of student work

- Annotated examples of student work showing what has been done well and what could be improved

- Exemplar pieces of work illustrating what needs to be done to achieve certain grades

- Checklists, wordlists and other tools which pupils can refer to during lessons

- Displays containing material connected to the current topics of study

Health and Safety

37 One of the legal responsibilities incumbent on all schools is to look after the health and safety of pupils and staff.

If there is a health and safety issue in your classroom, or any area of the school for that matter, you should ask for it to be dealt with immediately, regardless of whether an inspection is impending or not.

Should inspectors come to the school and see a health and safety issue, this will reflect badly on all involved.

Can you move around with ease?

38 We turn now to think about various aspects of any lessons you might teach, as well as websites from which you can garner useful information.

To begin, let us ask this question: When you are teaching, can you move around with ease?

If you can't, then this is less than ideal. Maybe you should rearrange the layout of your classroom, amend your seating plan or see if you can be moved to a larger room. I draw your attention to this point because it is something that could hinder or frustrate you if you are being observed.

For example, it is good to circulate during a lesson so that you can talk to students, elicit information about their learning and keep them on task. If you cannot move around the room with ease, for whatever reason, these benefits will be harder to come by.

Tinker with your Seating Plans

39 Tinkering with seating plans is an absolutely excellent thing to do. Refining, adapting and altering them based on the information you elicit while teaching should lead to better outcomes.

However, don't forget to amend the electronic copies of your seating plans. After all, you don't want to hand an inspector a seating plan which is out of date!

Have a Back-Up!

40 Sometimes, things go wrong. Perhaps worst of all, the technology might fail. This can be incredibly annoying.

That annoyance is a function of the fact that we have been frustrated in our attempts to reach a goal. It is also connected to the sense of not being in control of what is happening.

To avoid such emotions (which are unhelpful, especially if they appear during an observation), have a back-up ready. Planning what to do if problems occur is a great way to avoid problems. Because, if you have a plan ready, the problem ceases to be problematic.

Ofsted.gov.uk

41 When preparing for Ofsted, it is always worth visiting their website – http://www.ofsted.gov.uk/schools. Here you will find a range of resources (some of which we will look at in more detail in the following entries).

These include:

- Inspection reports

- Latest news

- Frequently asked questions

- Official documentation

- The framework for school inspection

The website is well-designed and easy to navigate and search. As the old saying goes, knowledge is power. Priming yourself using the Ofsted website is thus a good step on the path to preparing for an inspection.

The Current Inspection Framework

42 At the time of writing (April 2014), the current inspection framework can be found at https://www.gov.uk/government/publications/the-framework-for-school-inspection. This is available in PDF and Word format.

Should you be reading this at a much later date and the link not work, simply search 'The framework for school inspection' in the search box on Ofsted's website.

The framework for school inspection "sets out how the general principles and processes of inspection are applied to maintained schools and several other types of school in England. It states the statutory basis for inspection and summarises the main features of school inspections carried out under section 5 of the Education Act 2005 from September 2012." (taken from http://www.ofsted.gov.uk/resources/framework-for-school-inspection, accessed in April 2014)

It is therefore useful reading if you are preparing for an inspection.

Good Practice Guides

43 One of the lesser known facts about Ofsted is that they actually produce a wide selection of good practice guides. You can find these at http://archive.excellencegateway.org.uk/goodpractic edatabase.

The page allows you to search for different types of material connected to schools.

To give an example of the wonderful things hidden away in this part of the site, here are the top five resources which came up when I searched:

- High-quality alternative provision through a consortium of schools (Saffron Walden County High School)

- Early years good practice films – various examples

- A guide to nursery transition focussing on Ann Tayler Children's Centre Nursery

- Raising standards through high-quality leadership of teaching: St Mary's Church of England Voluntary Controlled Primary School

- Helping families and children get ready for school: Mayflower Primary School

And that was only covering April 3rd 2014 – April 24th 2014!

Specific Guidance

44 Ofsted also offer specific guidance on their website. For example, you can find a whole host of documents covering subject-specific guidance for inspectors making judgements during subject survey visits to schools. Simply visit: https://www.gov.uk/schools-colleges-childrens-services/inspections.

Guidance of this type is extremely helpful in getting a sense of what outstanding practice means and some of the ways in which inspectors are being asked to make judgements. While nothing is ever set in stone, guidance documents can be just that – a guide to help you prepare effectively.

Outstanding Inspection Reports

45 Another tool at your disposal through the Ofsted website is inspection results from schools which have been graded outstanding. If you know of a school in the local area which has received such a rating, have a look at their inspection report and see what information you can glean from it.

On some occasions, outstanding reports may not be hugely helpful to you. On other occasions, they can be a great aid. Have a look at a few to see whether they work for you. The webpage for searching can be found at http://reports.ofsted.gov.uk/.

Ofsted also produce a list of outstanding providers which you can access at https://www.gov.uk/government/statistical-data-sets/outstanding-providers-2013-14.

Relax

46 We draw the book to a close by attending to a few more general points which can assist you in your preparations for an inspection.

This is the first one: relax.

I know it's difficult (I've been through a fair few inspections myself) but if you are relaxed you are far more likely to perform better.

It's no good just telling yourself to relax, though. Often, that doesn't work. Instead, try doing these things:

- Prepare yourself

- Get any materials you need ready

- Make a note of what you need to know or do during the inspection

- Ensure you have a lesson back-up, just in case

- Eat healthily

Doing these things will make it easier for you to relax.

If you're prepared, then you're prepared

47 Which leads me on to this point:

If you're prepared, you're prepared. If you've done everything you need to do, then you don't need to do any more.

So relax.

Speak to Colleagues

48 Speaking to colleagues is a great way to maintain a sense of perspective, gain vital support and generally feel like you're all in it together. What is more, you will be able to share thoughts, run ideas past one another and identify any potential problems or solutions.

While everyone is likely to be very busy around the time of an inspection (or during the days in which people believe an inspection to be imminent), don't let this prevent you from having a chat. And, if possible, have a laugh and a joke as well! This will make everyone feel better and bring a bit of levity to proceedings.

Know Your Strengths (And Play to Them)

49 Let's face it, if you bought this book then you're a good teacher. I can say this because it demonstrates that you want to achieve highly and do the best for your students. After all, you have gone out of your way to read advice on how to prepare for an inspection.

From these facts we can deduce that you have strengths and that there are many things you do as a teacher which are good. Maybe there are even hundreds of things! Probably there are.

So play to these strengths. Make a virtue out of them. Use them to your advantage and to the advantage of your pupils if you are being observed (or even if you are just speaking to an inspector). Show them that you are professional, hard-working and good at your job.

It's All About Learning and Progress

50 Let us conclude by revisiting the central theme of this book. Inspections are concerned with whether students are safe and well looked after and whether they are making the very best progress possible.

This is what schools are for – to make learning happen.

Retain these thoughts in the forefront of your mind and you will have an excellent lens through which to look at what you are doing. And this is not just true of the period preceding and during an inspection. It is true at all times.

Ultimately, if you want to prepare for an inspection you should do all the things which constitute good practice and which make great learning happen.

And if you want more advice and guidance on any areas of outstanding teaching and learning, see my other books, visit my website for plenty of free resources, or get in touch.

And if you do get inspected: Good luck!

A Brief Request

If you have found this book useful I would be delighted if you could leave a review on Amazon to let others know.

If you have any thoughts or comments, or if you have an idea for a new book in the series you would like me to write, please don't hesitate to get in touch at mike@mikegershon.com.

Finally, don't forget that you can download all my teaching and learning resources for **FREE** at www.mikegershon.com.